GRANNY STITCH
Blankets

GRANNY STITCH
Blankets

10 Fresh and Modern Granny Throws That Go Way Beyond the Iconic Square

SALENA BACA

Stackpole Books
Essex, Connecticut
Blue Ridge Summit, Pennsylvania

STACKPOLE BOOKS
An imprint of The Globe Pequot Publishing Group, Inc.
64 South Main Street
Essex, CT 06426
www.globepequot.com
Distributed by NATIONAL BOOK NETWORK
800-462-6420

Copyright © 2025 Salena Baca

Photography by Tambi Lane, www.tambilanephoto.com

All rights reserved. No part of this book may be reproduced in any form or by any electronic or mechanical means, including information storage and retrieval systems, without written permission from the publisher, except by a reviewer who may quote passages in a review.

The contents of this book are for personal use only. Patterns herein may be reproduced in limited quantities for such use. Any large-scale commercial reproduction is prohibited without the written consent of the publisher.

We have made every effort to ensure the accuracy and completeness of these instructions. We cannot, however, be responsible for human error, typographical mistakes, or variations in individual work.

British Library Cataloguing in Publication Information available

Library of Congress Cataloging-in-Publication Data available

ISBN 978-0-8117-7543-4 (paper : alk. paper)
ISBN 978-0-8117-7544-1 (electronic)

First Edition

∞™ The paper used in this publication meets the minimum requirements of American National Standard for Information Sciences—Permanence of Paper for Printed Library Materials, ANSI/NISO Z39.48-1992.

Contents

Introduction   6
Stitch Key   6

Basic Stitch Granny Throw
7

Corner-to-Corner Granny Throw
10

Criss Cross Granny Throw
12

Granny Hexagon Throw
14

Granny Rectangles Throw
18

Granny Scrap Throw
21

Granny Square Reflections Throw
24

Granny Triangles Throw
26

Lazy Days Throw
29

Mile-a-Minute Granny Throw
32

Resources   34

Introduction

When I was young, the first thing I learned to crochet was a granny square. Our teacher showed us how in class, then stitched all our little squares together into blankets for the community. No wonder the granny square became such a classic—it's easy to learn, fun to make, and comes together into something warm and cozy before you know it.

I've loved granny squares for as long as I can remember, but after years of crocheting them, I wanted to make some changes. That's why this book features fresh takes on the classic—no boring repeats here! You'll find everything from squares and triangles to hexagons, chevrons, and even diamonds worked corner to corner.

I played around with texture and color, mixing different yarn types and shades to make unique combinations. I also used chunky yarns for quick projects and even a super-bulky yarn to make a weighted blanket. Each design is throw-sized—perfect for baby blankets, lap covers, or adding a crafty touch to your couch or bed. And since most of these projects are worked in pieces, they're easy to take on the go. If you've got a soft spot for granny squares like I do, I hope the designs in this book add a whole new level of joy and creativity to your crochet life!

**Peace + Love + Crochet,
Salena Baca**

Stitch Key

ch(s) = chain(s)
dc = double crochet
hdc = half double crochet
sc = single crochet

Sl st = slip stitch
st(s) = stitch(es)
tr = triple/treble crochet

Basic Stitch Granny Throw

This throw is all about mixing it up! Classic granny squares meet triangles to form the perfect square. Each motif follows the same color pattern, which adds depth and dimension to this otherwise simple design. It's a fresh spin on a classic!

YARN
Lion Brand Basic Stitch Thick & Quick Anti-Microbial, bulky #5 (65% recycled polyester, 35% Amicor acrylic; 87 yds./80 m per 3.5 oz./100 g skein)
Color A: Smoke, 7 skeins
Color B: Charcoal, 6 skeins
Color C: Cement, 8 skeins

TOOLS
US size L/11 (8 mm) crochet hook
Yarn needle

GAUGE
Square = 25 in./63.5 cm diagonally, corner to corner
Triangle = 12.5 in./31.75 cm tall x 25 in./63.5 cm wide

FINISHED SIZE
Without border: 50 in./127 cm wide x 50 in./127 cm tall
Border adds extra 1.5 in./3.75 cm

PATTERN NOTES
- Throw is worked by creating Squares (rounds) and Triangles (rows) that are crocheted together once complete.
- The contrasting colors help to feature the construction of the individual pieces, while adding a dimension to what would otherwise be a basic square.
- To replicate color changes shown in example, work as follows:

Square: Color A = Rounds 1–6, Color B = Rounds 7–9, Color C = Rounds 10–12
Triangle: Color A = Rows 1–6, Color B = Rows 7–9, Color C = Rows 10–12

INSTRUCTIONS

Granny Square (make 4)
Round 1 (right side): Ch 4, skip 3 ch (first dc), work the following into the 4th ch: 2 dc, ch 2, [3 dc, ch 2] 3 times. Sl St into top of beginning ch-3 to join—20 sts; 12 dc + 4 ch-2 spaces.

Round 2: Sl st into each of next 2 dc, Sl st into ch-2 space, ch 3 (first dc, here and throughout), (2 dc, ch 2, 3 dc) into same ch-2 space, ch 1, [(3 dc, ch 2, 3 dc) into next ch-2 space, ch 1] 3 times, Sl st into top of beginning ch-3 to join—36 sts; 24 dc + 4 ch-2 spaces + 4 ch-1 spaces.

Round 3: Sl st into each of next 2 dc, Sl st into ch-2 space, (ch 3, 2 dc, ch 2, 3 dc) into same ch-2 space, ch 1, (3 dc, ch 1) into ch-1 space, [(3 dc, ch 2, 3 dc) into next ch-2 space, ch 1, (3 dc, ch 1) into ch-1 space] 3 times, Sl st into top of beginning ch-3 to join—52 sts; 36 dc + 4 ch-2 spaces + 8 ch-1 spaces.

Round 4: Sl st into each of next 2 dc, Sl st into ch-2 space, (ch 3, 2 dc, ch 2, 3 dc) into same ch-2 space, ch 1, (3 dc, ch 1) into each ch-1 space, [(3 dc, ch 2, 3 dc) into next ch-2 space, ch 1, (3 dc, ch 1) into each ch-1 space] 3 times, Sl st into top of beginning ch-3 to join—68 sts; 48 dc + 4 ch-2 spaces + 12 ch-1 spaces.

Repeat Round 4 until 12 rounds are complete, adding 12 sts to each new round of work, ending with 196 sts; 144 dc + 4 ch-2 spaces + 44 ch. Fasten off.

Granny Triangle (make 8)
Row 1 (right side): Ch 5 (first dc, ch-1 space, base ch), (3 dc, ch 2, 3 dc, ch 1, dc) into 5th ch from hook—12 sts; 8 dc + 4 ch.

Row 2: Ch 4 (first dc and ch-1 space), turn, (3 dc, ch 1) into ch-1 space, (3 dc, ch 2, 3 dc) into ch-2 space, (ch 1, 3 dc) into ch-1 space, (ch 1, dc) into top of last st in row—20 sts; 14 dc + 6 ch.

Row 3: Ch 4, turn, (3 dc, ch 1) into next 2 ch-1 spaces, (3 dc, ch 2, 3 dc) into ch-2 space, (ch 1, 3 dc) into next 2 ch-1 spaces, (ch 1, dc) into top of last st in row—28 sts; 20 dc + 8 ch.

Row 4: Ch 4, turn, (3 dc, ch 1) into next 3 ch-1 spaces, (3 dc, ch 2, 3 dc) into ch-2 space, (ch 1, 3 dc) into next 3 ch-1 spaces, (ch 1, dc) into top of last st in row—36 sts; 26 dc + 10 ch.

Row 5: Ch 4, turn, (3 dc, ch 1) into next 4 ch-1 spaces, (3 dc, ch 2, 3 dc) into ch-2 space, (ch 1, 3 dc) into next 4 ch-1 spaces, (ch 1, dc) into top of last st in row—44 sts; 32 dc + 12 ch.

Row 6: Ch 4, turn, (3 dc, ch 1) into next 5 ch-1 spaces, (3 dc, ch 2, 3 dc) into ch-2 space, (ch 1, 3 dc) into next 5 ch-1 spaces, (ch 1, dc) into top of last st in row—52 sts; 38 dc + 14 ch.

Row 7: Ch 4, turn, (3 dc, ch 1) into next 6 ch-1 spaces, (3 dc, ch 2, 3 dc) into ch-2 space, (ch 1, 3 dc) into next 6 ch-1 spaces, (ch 1, dc) into top of last st in row—60 sts; 44 dc + 16 ch.

Row 8: Ch 4, turn, (3 dc, ch 1) into next 7 ch-1 spaces, (3 dc, ch 2, 3 dc) into ch-2 space, (ch 1, 3 dc) into next 7 ch-1 spaces, (ch 1, dc) into top of last st in row—68 sts; 50 dc + 18 ch.

Row 9: Ch 4, turn, (3 dc, ch 1) into next 8 ch-1 spaces, (3 dc, ch 2, 3 dc) into ch-2 space, (ch 1, 3 dc) into next 8 ch-1 spaces, (ch 1, dc) into top of last st in row—76 sts; 56 dc + 20 ch.

Row 10: Ch 4, turn, (3 dc, ch 1) into next 9 ch-1 spaces, (3 dc, ch 2, 3 dc) into ch-2 space, (ch 1, 3 dc) into next 9 ch-1 spaces, (ch 1, dc) into top of last st in row—84 sts; 62 dc + 22 ch.

Row 11: Ch 4, turn, (3 dc, ch 1) into next 10 ch-1 spaces, (3 dc, ch 2, 3 dc) into ch-2 space, (ch 1, 3 dc) into next 10 ch-1 spaces, (ch 1, dc) into top of last st in row—92 sts; 68 dc + 24 ch.

Row 12: Ch 4, turn, (3 dc, ch 1) into next 11 ch-1 spaces, (3 dc, ch 2, 3 dc) into ch-2 space, (ch 1, 3 dc) into next 11 ch-1 spaces, (ch 1, dc) into top of last st in row—100 sts; 74 dc + 26 ch.

Seams
With Right Sides of all square and triangle motifs facing the same direction, arrange into the pattern shown in the diagram. Seams will be worked through both pieces of fabric held together.

Seam 1
With Color C, pull up a loop into ch-1 spaces from final row of Triangles 1 and 2.
Row 1 (right side): Sc, *ch 3, skip 3 sts, sc into next ch space*, repeat from * to * across 1 side each of: Triangles 1 and 2, Squares 1 and 2, Squares 3 and 4, Triangles 5 and 6. Fasten off.

Seam 2
With Color C, pull up a loop into ch-1 space from final row of Triangle 8 and corresponding ch-2 space from final round of Square 1.
Row 1 (right side): Sc, *ch 3, skip 3 sts, sc into next ch space*, repeat from * to * across 1 side each of: Triangle 8 and Square 1, Triangle 7 and Square 4. Fasten off.

Seam 3
With Color C, pull up a loop into ch-1 space from final row of Triangle 3 and corresponding ch-2 space from final round of Square 2.
Row 1 (right side): Sc, *ch 3, skip 3 sts, sc into next ch space*, repeat from * to * across 1 side each of: Triangle 3 and Square 2, Triangle 4 and Square 3. Fasten off.

Seam 4
With Color C, pull up a loop into ch-1 spaces from final row of Triangles 3 and 4.
Row 1 (right side): Sc, *ch 3, skip 3 sts, sc into next ch- space*, repeat from * to * across 1 side each of: Triangles 3 and 4, Squares 2 and 3, Squares 1 and 4, Triangles 7 and 8. Fasten off.

Seam 5
With Color C, pull up a loop into ch-1 space from final row of Triangle 5 and corresponding ch-2 space from final round of Square 3.
Row 1 (right side): Sc, *ch 3, skip 3 sts, sc into next ch space*, repeat from * to * across 1 side each of: Triangle 5 and Square 3, Triangle 6 and Square 4. Fasten off.

Seam 6
With Color C, pull up a loop into ch-1 space from final row of Triangle 2 and corresponding ch-2 space from final round of Square 2.
Row 1 (right side): Sc, *ch 3, skip 3 sts, sc into next ch space*, repeat from * to * across 1 side each of: Triangle 2 and Square 2, Triangle 1 and Square 1. Fasten off.

Border
Assure right side of throw is facing. With Color A, pull up a loop into side of last st in last row of Triangle 1.
Round 1 (right side): Ch 2 (not a st), work 2 hdc into same space, work 3 hdc into every side of st in Triangle rows around border, Sl st into top of first st to join, fasten off—576 hdc.

Finishing
Sew in all ends, trim excess.

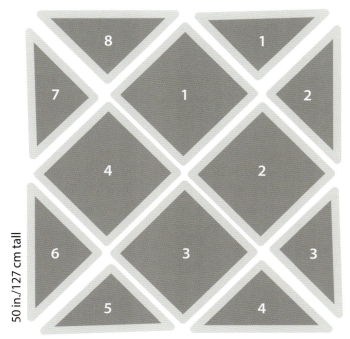

50 in./127 cm wide
50 in./127 cm tall

18 in./45.75 cm wide
18 in./45.75 cm tall
25 in./63.5 cm diagonally

25 in./63.5 cm wide
12.5in./31.75 cm tall

Corner-to-Corner Granny Throw

You'll make this square with a classic granny stitch, working back and forth in simple rows. The blanket starts at one corner, growing into a triangle as rows are added. Once you have half the size you want, you'll decrease each row until your triangle becomes a square. Using a solid and a variegated yarn together creates a thicker texture and a cool, custom color blend!

YARN
Lion Brand Fishermen's Wool, medium #4 (100% wool; 465 yds./425 m per 8 oz./227 g skein)
Color A: Oatmeal, 3 skeins

Lion Brand Scarfie, bulky #5 (78% acrylic, 22% wool; 312 yds./285 m per 5.3 oz./150 g skein)
Color B: Taupe/Charcoal, 3 skeins

TOOLS
US size L/11 (8 mm) crochet hook
Yarn needle

GAUGE
8 pattern rows = 7 in./17.75 cm
23 pattern sts = 10 in./25.5 cm

FINISHED SIZE
Without Border: 43 in./109.25 cm across square, or 60 in./152.5 cm diagonally, corner to corner
Border adds 3 in./7.5 cm to total measurements

SPECIALTY STITCH
Dc3tog (dc 3 sts together; decrease): [Yarn over, insert hook into st or space, yarn over, pull through st or space, yarn over, pull through 2 loops] 3 times, yarn over, pull through all loops.

PATTERN NOTES
- Blanket is worked with two strands of yarn (Colors A and B) held together. Border is worked with two strands of Color A held together.

- This pattern is created in a diamond shape. Begin at one corner, increasing the stitch count every row until reaching half the desired blanket size. Then, decrease the stitch count every row until the diamond (square) is formed.

INSTRUCTIONS

Blanket
Row 1: With Colors A and B held together, ch 5 (first dc, ch-1 space, base ch), (3 dc, ch 1, dc) into 5th ch from hook—7 sts; 5 dc + 2 ch.
Row 2: Ch 4 (first dc and ch-1 space), turn, (3 dc, ch 1) into each ch-1 space, dc into top of last st in row—11 sts; 8 dc + 3 ch.
Repeat Row 2 until 34 rows are complete, adding 3 dc and 1 ch per row, ending with 139 sts; 104 dc + 35 ch.
Row 35: Ch 3 (first dc), turn, work 3 dc into first ch-1 space, (ch 1, 3 dc) into remaining ch-1 spaces across, dc into top of last st in row—141 sts; 107 dc + 34 ch.
The first half of the blanket is now complete, and every row will now decrease until the diamond (square) is formed.
Row 36: Ch 4, turn, (3 dc, ch 1) into each ch-1 space across, dc into top of last st in row—139 sts; 104 dc + 35 ch.
Row 37: Ch 4, turn, skip first ch-1 space, (3 dc, ch 1) into each ch-1 space across until 1 remains, skip last ch-1 space, dc into top of last st in row—135 sts; 101 dc + 34 ch.
Repeat Row 37 until 69 rows are complete, decreasing 3 dc and 1 ch per row, ending with 7 sts; 5 dc + 2 ch.
Row 70: Ch 3, turn, skip first ch-1 space, dc3tog, skip last ch-1 space, dc into top of last st in row, fasten off—3 sts; 2 dc + 1 dc3tog.

Border
Join yarn into side of last dc from Row 70.
Round 1 (right side): With 2 strands of Color A held together ch 1 (not a st, here and throughout), work 3 sc around each dc row end, Sl st into top of first sc to join—420 sc.
Rounds 2–3: Ch 1, sc into each st around, Sl st into top of first sc to join—420 sc.
Fasten off after last row complete.

Finishing
Sew in all ends, trim excess..

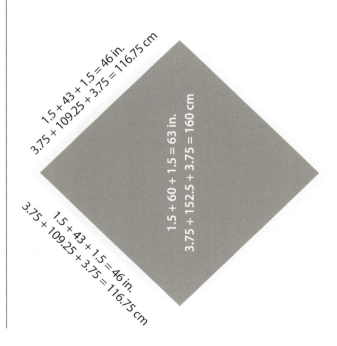

CORNER-TO-CORNER GRANNY THROW

Criss Cross Granny Throw

This throw blanket follows the same basic stitch pattern as the Corner-to-Corner Granny Throw but adds a unique design with alternating colors. When you seam together four completed squares, the color changes create a striking cross pattern at the center.

YARN
Lion Brand Hue + Me, bulky #5 (80% acrylic, 20% wool; 137 yds./125 m per 4.4 oz./125 g skein)
Color A: Sea Glass, 6 skeins
Color B: Salt, 6 skeins

TOOLS
US size K/10.5 (6.5 mm) crochet hook
Yarn needle

GAUGE
4 pattern rows = 4 in./10.25 cm
11 pattern sts = 4 in./10.25 cm

FINISHED SIZE
Without Border: 50 in./127 cm across square, or 72 in./183 cm diagonally, corner to corner
Border adds 1.5 in./3.75 cm to total measurements

SPECIALTY STITCH
Dc3tog (dc 3 sts together; decrease): [Yarn over, insert hook into st or space, yarn over, pull through st or space, yarn over, pull through 2 loops] 3 times, yarn over, pull through all loops.

PATTERN NOTES
- Blanket is worked by creating 4 squares (rows) that are seamed together (rows), with a border added last (round).
- Each square is created in a diamond shape, beginning at one corner and increasing the stitch count every row until reaching half the desired size, then decreasing the stitch count every row until the diamond (square) is formed.

- The "criss cross" pattern is prevalent because each square has the same color striping, arranged to create the visual effect shown. Lay out each square until the criss cross pattern is shown before seaming together.

INSTRUCTIONS

Square (Make 4)
Use Color A first for 2 rows, then change to Color B for 2 rows. Repeat this color pattern for the remainder of Square (ending with 2 rows of Color B). Do not fasten off colors; carry them as you work.

Row 1 (right side): Ch 5 (first dc, ch-1 space, base ch), (3 dc, ch 1, dc) into 5th ch from hook—7 sts; 5 dc + 2 ch.

Row 2: Ch 4 (first dc and ch-1 space), turn, (3 dc, ch 1) into each ch-1 space, dc into top of last st in row—11 sts; 8 dc + 3 ch.

Repeat Row 2 until 22 rows are complete, adding 3 dc and 1 ch per row, ending with 91 sts; 68 dc + 23 ch.

Row 23: Ch 3 (first dc), turn, work 3 dc into first ch-1 space, (ch 1, 3 dc) into remaining ch-1 spaces across, dc into top of last st in row—93 sts; 71 dc + 22 ch.

The first half of the Square is complete, and every row will now decrease until the diamond (square) is formed.

Row 24: Ch 4, turn, (3 dc, ch 1) into each ch-1 space across, dc into top of last st in row—91 sts; 68 dc + 23 ch.

Row 25: Ch 4, turn, skip first ch-1 space, (3 dc, ch 1) into each ch-1 space across until 1 remains, skip last ch-1 space, dc into top of last st in row—87 sts; 65 dc + 22 ch.

Repeat Row 25 until 45 rows are complete, decreasing 3 dc and 1 ch per row, ending with 7 sts; 5 dc + 2 ch.

Row 46: Ch 3, turn, skip first ch-1 space, dc3tog, skip last ch-1 space, dc into top of last st in row, fasten off—3 sts; 2 dc + 1 dc3tog.

Seams
With the right sides facing the same direction, hold any two squares together along one side, from Row 1 through Row 23.

Seam is worked by alternating sc sts from the side of one square to the side of the adjacent square, connecting them together.

Row 1 (right side): Starting in Row 1 of Square 1 and Row 1 of Square 2 *[sc around side of dc of Square 1, sc around side of dc of Square 2] 2 times*, repeat from * to * for Rows 2–23, working from Square 1 to Square 2 (92 sc). With the right sides facing the same direction, hold 2 remaining Squares together along one side (starting in Row 23). Repeat from * to * for Rows 23–1, working from Square 3 to Square 4 (92 sc). Fasten off—184 sc.

Rotate Squares to work along unjoined sides. Repeat Row 1.

Border
With right sides of Squares and Seams facing, join yarn into the side of any dc along outer edge.

Round 1 (right side): With Color A ch 2 (first st), work 3 hdc into side of each dc along outer edge, Sl st to join, fasten off—552 hdc.

Finishing
Sew in all ends, trim excess.

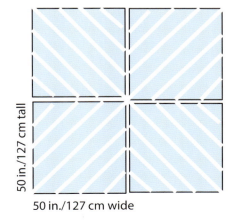

50 in./127 cm tall

50 in./127 cm wide

25 in./63.5 cm tall

25 in./63.5 cm wide

Granny Hexagon Throw

Granny squares? Think again—this blanket is all about granny hexagons! Every hexagon motif is seamlessly slip-stitched to the next as you crochet, so there's zero sewing involved when you join (just a few ends when you're done). And with a bold, contrasting border around each one, those hexagon shapes really pop!

YARN
Lion Brand Wool-Ease Thick & Quick, super bulky #6 (80% acrylic, 20% wool; 87 yds./80 m per 5 oz./140 g skein)
Color A: Fossil, 9 skeins

Lion Brand Hue + Me, bulky #5 (80% acrylic, 20% wool; 137 yds./125 m per 4.4 oz./125 g skein)
Color B: Saffron, 2 skeins

TOOLS
US size M/13 (9 mm) crochet hook
Stitch markers (to mark stitches, as desired)
Yarn needle

GAUGE
8-round Hexagon Motif = 18 in./45.75 cm across x 16 in./40.75 cm tall
8-row Half Hexagon Motif = 18 in./45.75 cm across x 8 in./20.25 cm tall

FINISHED SIZE
56 in./142.25 cm across x 50 in./127 cm tall (with border)

PATTERN NOTES
- Throw is created by joining individual hexagon and half hexagon motifs together.
- Hexagons (rounds) are created and joined first, then Half Hexagons (rows) are created and joined, finally a border is added.
- When joining motifs, the slip stitch join replaces 1 chain stitch in the current motif with 1 slip stitch into the joining motif. Refer to diagram on page 17 for placement of each motif.

INSTRUCTIONS

Hexagon 1

Round 1 (right side): With Color A ch 4, skip 3 ch (first dc), dc, ch 1, [2 dc, ch 1] 5 times into 4th ch from hook, Sl st into top of first dc to join—18 sts; 12 dc + 6 ch.

Round 2: Sl st into next st, Sl st into ch-1 space, ch 3 (first dc), (dc, ch 1, 2 dc) into ch-1 space, (2 dc, ch 1, 2 dc) into each ch-1 space around, Sl st into top of first dc to join—30 sts; 24 dc + 6 ch.

Round 3: Sl st into next st, Sl st into ch-1 space, ch 3 (first dc), (dc, ch 1, 2 dc) into ch-1 space, skip 2 sts, work 2 dc between sts, [(2 dc, ch 1, 2 dc) into next ch-1 space, skip 2 sts, work 2 dc between sts] 5 times, Sl st into top of first dc to join—42 sts; 36 dc + 6 ch.

Round 4: Sl st into next st, Sl st into ch-1 space, ch 3 (first dc), (dc, ch 1, 2 dc) into ch-1 space, [skip 2 sts, work 2 dc between sts] 2 times, *(2 dc, ch 1, 2 dc) into next ch-1 space, [skip 2 sts, work 2 dc between sts] 2 times*, repeat 5 times from * to *, Sl st into top of first dc to join—54 sts; 48 dc + 6 ch.

Round 5: Sl st into next st, Sl st into ch-1 space, ch 3 (first dc), (dc, ch 1, 2 dc) into ch-1 space, [skip 2 sts, work 2 dc between sts] 3 times, *(2 dc, ch 1, 2 dc) into next ch-1 space, [skip 2 sts, work 2 dc between sts] 3 times*, repeat 5 times from * to *, Sl st into top of first dc to join—66 sts; 60 dc + 6 ch.

Round 6: Sl st into next st, Sl st into ch-1 space, ch 3 (first dc), (dc, ch 1, 2 dc) into ch-1 space, [skip 2 sts, work 2 dc between sts] 4 times, *(2 dc, ch 1, 2 dc) into next ch-1 space, [skip 2 sts, work 2 dc between sts] 4 times*, repeat 5 times from * to *, Sl st into top of first dc to join—78 sts; 72 dc + 6 ch.

Round 7: Sl st into next st, Sl st into ch-1 space, ch 3 (first dc), (dc, ch 1, 2 dc) into ch-1 space, [skip 2 sts, work 2 dc between sts] 5 times, *(2 dc, ch 1, 2 dc) into next ch-1 space, [skip 2 sts, work 2 dc between sts] 5 times*, repeat 5 times from * to *, Sl st into top of first dc to join—90 sts; 84 dc + 6 ch.

Round 8: Sl st into next st, Sl st into ch-1 space, fasten off Color A, with Color B ch 3 (first dc), (dc, ch 1, 2 dc) into ch-1 space, [skip 2 sts, work 2 dc between sts] 6 times, *(2 dc, ch 1, 2 dc) into next ch-1 space, [skip 2 sts, work 2 dc between sts] 6 times*, repeat 5 times from * to *, Sl st into top of first dc to join, fasten off—102 sts; 96 dc + 6 ch.

Hexagon 2

Work Rounds 1–7 as for Hexagon 1; review diagram for placement and joining order.

Round 8: Work Round 8 as for Hexagon 1, except join into Hexagon 1 by replacing first 2 consecutive ch-1 spaces with Sl sts, and Sl st between each 2 dc group of adjoining motif along same side.

Hexagon 3

Work Rounds 1–7 as for Hexagon 1; review diagram for placement and joining order.

Round 8: Work Round 8 as for Hexagon 1, except join into Hexagon 2 along side 4 by replacing first 2 consecutive ch-1 spaces with Sl sts, and Sl st between each 2 dc group of adjoining motif along same side.

Hexagon 4

Work Rounds 1–8 as for Hexagon 1.

Hexagon 5

Work as for Hexagon 2, joining into Hexagon 4.

Hexagon 6

Work as for Hexagon 3, joining into Hexagon 5.

Hexagon 7

Work Rounds 1–7 as for Hexagon 1; review diagram for placement and joining order.

Round 8: Work Round 8 as for Hexagon 1, except join into Hexagon 1 (side 5) by replacing first *2 consecutive ch-1 spaces with Sl sts, and Sl st between each 2 dc group of adjoining motif along same side*, repeat from * to * along Hexagon 2 (side 6), work next side per pattern Round 8, repeat from *

GRANNY HEXAGON THROW 15

to * along Hexagon 5 (side 2) and Hexagon 4 (side 3), complete last side per pattern Round 8.

Hexagon 8
Work Rounds 1–7 as for Hexagon 1; review diagram for placement and joining order.

Round 8: Work Round 8 as for Hexagon 1, except join into Hexagon 6 (side 2) by replacing first *2 consecutive ch-1 spaces with Sl sts, and Sl st between each 2 dc group of adjoining motif along same side*, repeat from * to * along Hexagon 5 (side 3), Hexagon 7 (side 4), Hexagon 2 (side 5), Hexagon 3 (side 6), complete last side per pattern Round 8.

Half Hexagon 1
Row 1: With Color A ch 4, skip 3 ch (first dc), dc, [ch 1, 2 dc] 2 times—8 sts; 6 dc + 2 ch.

Row 2: Ch 3 (first dc, here and throughout), turn, dc into same st, [(2 dc, ch 1, 2 dc) into ch-1 space, skip 2 sts] 2 times, work 2 dc into top of last st—14 sts; 12 dc + 2 ch.

Row 3: Ch 3, turn, dc into same st, skip 1 st, work 2 dc between sts, [(2 dc, ch 1, 2 dc) into next ch-1 space, skip 2 sts, work 2 dc between sts] 2 times, work 2 dc into top of last st—20 sts; 18 dc + 2 ch.

Row 4: Ch 3, turn, dc into same st, skip 1 st, [work 2 dc between sts, skip 2 sts] 2 times, *(2 dc, ch 1, 2 dc) into next ch-1 space, [skip 2 sts, work 2 dc between sts] 2 times*, repeat 2 times from * to *, work 2 dc into top of last st—26 sts; 24 dc + 2 ch.

Row 5: Ch 3, turn, dc into same st, skip 1 st, [work 2 dc between sts, skip 2 sts] 3 times, *(2 dc, ch 1, 2 dc) into next ch-1 space, [skip 2 sts, work 2 dc between sts] 3 times*, repeat 2 times from * to *, work 2 dc into top of last st—32 sts; 30 dc + 2 ch.

Row 6: Ch 3, turn, dc into same st, skip 1 st, [work 2 dc between sts, skip 2 sts] 4 times, *(2 dc, ch 1, 2 dc) into next ch-1 space, [skip 2 sts, work 2 dc between sts] 4 times*, repeat 2 times from * to *, work 2 dc into top of last st—38 sts; 36 dc + 2 ch.

Row 7: Ch 3, turn, dc into same st, skip 1 st, [work 2 dc between sts, skip 2 sts] 5 times, *(2 dc, ch 1, 2 dc) into next ch-1 space, [skip 2 sts, work 2 dc between sts] 5 times*, repeat 2 times from * to *, work 2 dc into top of last st, fasten off Color A—44 sts; 42 dc + 2 ch.

Attach Color B yarn between last 2 dc from Row 7. Turn to work into sides of rows. Work the next as a round.

Round 8 (right side): Ch 3 (first dc), dc into same st, work 2 dc into sides of next 12 rows, (2 dc, Sl st into ch-1 space between sides 1 and 6 of Hexagon 1, 2 dc) into last row, skip 2 sts from Hexagon 1, Sl st, skip 1 st in Row 7, work 2 dc between sts, [skip 2 sts from Hexagon 1, Sl st, skip 2 sts in Row 7, work 2 dc between sts] 5 times, skip 2 sts from Hexagon 1, Sl st, (2 dc, Sl st into ch-1 space between sides 1 and 2 of Hexagon 7, 2 dc) into next ch-1 space, [skip 2 sts from Hexagon 7, Sl st, skip 2 sts from Row 7, work 2 dc between sts] 6 times, skip 2 sts from Hexagon 7, Sl st, (2 dc, Sl st into ch-1 space between sides 2 and 3 of Hexagon 4, 2 dc) into next ch-1 space, [skip 2 sts from Hexagon 4, Sl st, skip 2 sts from Row 7, work 2 dc between sts] 6 times, skip 2 sts from Hexagon 4, Sl st, skip 1 st in Row 7, work 2 dc between sts, Sl st into ch-1 space between sides 1 and 2 of Hexagon 4, Sl st into top of first dc, fasten off—101 sts; 76 dc + 25 Sl st.

Half Hexagon 2
Work Rows 1–7 as for Half Hexagon 1. Attach Color B yarn between last 2 dc from Row 7. Turn to work into sides of rows.

Round 8 (right side): Ch 3 (first dc), dc into same st, work 2 dc into sides of next 12 Rows, (2 dc, Sl st into ch-1 space between sides 3 and 4 of Hexagon 6, 2 dc) into last row, skip 2 sts from Hexagon 6, Sl st, skip 1 st in Row 7, work 2 dc between sts, [skip 2 sts from Hexagon 6, Sl st, skip 2 sts in Row 7, work 2 dc between sts] 5 times, skip 2 sts from Hexagon 6, Sl st, (2 dc, Sl st into ch-1 space between sides 4 and 5 of Hexagon 8, 2 dc) into next ch-1 space, [skip 2 sts from Hexagon 8, Sl st, skip 2 sts from Row 7, work 2 dc between sts] 6 times, skip 2 sts from Hexagon 8, Sl st, (2 dc, Sl st into ch-1 space between sides 6 and 5 of Hexagon 3, 2 dc) into next ch-1 space, [skip 2 sts from Hexagon 3, Sl st, skip 2 sts from Row 7, work 2 dc between sts] 6 times, skip 2 sts from Hexagon 3, Sl st, skip 1 st in Row 7, work 2 dc between sts, Sl st into ch-1 space between sides 4 and 5 of Hexagon 3, Sl st into top of first dc, fasten off—101 sts; 76 dc + 25 Sl st.

Border

Round 1 (right side): Attach color B into first ch-1 space in side 1 of Hexagon 1, ch 3 (first dc), dc, work 2 dc between groups of 2 dc from previous round, (2 dc, ch 1, 2 dc) into ch-1 space between sides 1 and 2 of Hexagon 1 and ch-1 space between sides 2 and 3 of Hexagon 3, ch-1 space between sides 2 and 3 of Hexagon 2, ch-1 space between sides 1 and 6 of Hexagon 4, ch-1 space between sides 6 and 5 of Hexagon 6, ch-1 space between sides 6 and 5 of Hexagon 5—358 sts; 348 dc + 10 ch.

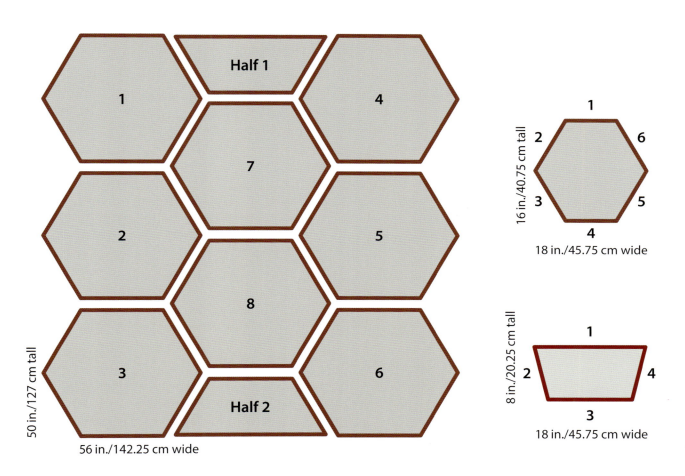

GRANNY HEXAGON THROW 17

Granny Rectangles Throw

Once you make the flexible foundation, you'll probably think this rectangle motif is easier than a granny square! After making two separate rectangles, you'll join a third between the first two with a simple slip stitch join as you work the last round. The mix of contrasting colors not only adds depth to this design, but also showcases the clever construction of this throw.

YARN
Lion Brand Jiffy, bulky #5 (100% acrylic; 681 yds./623 m per 14.5 oz./410 g skein)
Color A: Cream, 1 skein
Color B: Seafoam, 1 skein
Color C: Cedar, 1 skein

TOOLS
US size K/10.5 (6.5 mm) crochet hook
Stitch markers (to mark stitches, as desired)
Yarn needle

GAUGE
1 Granny Rectangle = 15 in./38 cm wide x 53 in./134.5 cm long (without fringe)

FINISHED SIZE
45 in./114.25 cm wide x 53 in./134.5 cm long (without fringe)

PATTERN NOTES
- Throw is worked by creating 3 individual Granny Rectangles (rounds), with the third being joined between the first two with crochet.
- Each rectangle is worked in two parts: Foundation (rows), Rectangle (rounds).
- The contrasting colors help to feature the construction.

INSTRUCTIONS

Rectangle Foundation
Row 1: With Color A ch 5, skip 4 ch (first tr), work 1 tr into next ch—2 tr.
Row 2: Ch 4 (first tr), turn, work 1 tr into next st—2 tr.
Repeat Row 2 until 30 rows are complete. Do not fasten off, continue to Rectangle.

Rectangle
Round 1 (right side): Ch 3 (first dc), turn, work 2 dc between tr sts from last row of Rectangle Foundation, *ch 3, rotate to work into sides of rows from Rectangle Foundation, work 3 dc into each of next 30 rows, ch 3*, rotate to work into Row 1 of Rectangle Foundation, work 3 dc between tr sts, repeat from * to * one time, Sl st into top of first dc to join—198 sts; 186 dc + 4 ch-3 spaces.

Round 2: Sl st into each of next 2 dc, Sl st into ch-3 space, ch 3 (first dc), (2 dc, ch 3, 3 dc) into same ch-3 space, *[skip 3 sts, work 3 dc between 3rd and 4th sts] 29 times, (3 dc, ch 3, 3 dc) into ch-3 space*, skip 3 sts, (3 dc, ch 3, 3 dc) into ch-3 space, repeat from * to * one time, Sl st into top of first dc to join—210 sts; 198 dc + 4 ch-3 spaces.

Round 3: Sl st into each of next 2 dc, Sl st into ch-3 space, ch 3 (first dc), (2 dc, ch 3, 3 dc) into same ch-3 space, *[skip 3 sts, work 3 dc between 3rd and 4th sts] 30 times, (3 dc, ch 3, 3 dc) into ch-3 space, skip 3 sts, work 3 dc between 3rd and 4th sts*, (3 dc, ch 3, 3 dc) into ch-3 space, repeat from * to * one time, Sl st into top of first dc to join—222 sts; 210 dc + 4 ch-3 spaces.

Round 4: Sl st into each of next 2 dc, Sl st into ch-3 space, ch 3 (first dc), (2 dc, ch 3, 3 dc) into same ch-3 space, *[skip 3 sts, work 3 dc between 3rd and 4th sts] 31 times, (3 dc, ch 3, 3 dc) into ch-3 space, [skip 3 sts, work 3 dc between 3rd and 4th sts] 2 times*, (3 dc, ch 3, 3 dc) into ch-3 space, repeat from * to * one time, Sl st into top of first dc to join—234 sts; 222 dc + 4 ch-3 spaces.

Round 5: Sl st into each of next 2 dc, Sl st into ch-3 space, ch 3 (first dc), (2 dc, ch 3, 3 dc) into same ch-3 space, *[skip 3 sts, work 3 dc between 3rd and 4th sts] 32 times, (3 dc, ch 3, 3 dc) into ch-3 space, [skip 3 sts, work 3 dc between 3rd and 4th sts] 3 times*, (3 dc, ch 3, 3 dc) into ch-3 space, repeat from * to * one time, Sl st into top of first dc to join—246 sts; 234 dc + 4 ch-3 spaces.

Round 6: Sl st into each of next 2 dc, Sl st into ch-3 space, fasten off Color A, with Color B ch 3 (first dc), (2 dc, ch 3, 3 dc) into same ch-3 space, *[skip 3 sts, work 3 dc between 3rd and 4th sts] 33 times, (3 dc, ch 3, 3 dc) into ch-3 space, [skip 3 sts, work 3 dc between 3rd and 4th sts] 4 times*, (3 dc, ch 3, 3 dc) into ch-3 space, repeat from * to * one time, Sl st into top of first dc to join—258 sts; 246 dc + 4 ch-3 spaces.

Round 7: Sl st into each of next 2 dc, Sl st into ch-3 space, ch 3 (first dc), (2 dc, ch 3, 3 dc) into same ch-3 space, *[skip 3 sts, work 3 dc between 3rd and 4th sts] 34 times, (3 dc, ch 3, 3 dc) into ch-3 space, [skip 3 sts, work 3 dc between 3rd and 4th sts] 5 times*, (3 dc, ch 3, 3 dc) into ch-3 space, repeat from * to * one time, Sl st into top of first dc to join—270 sts; 258 dc + 4 ch-3 spaces.

Round 8: Sl st into each of next 2 dc, Sl st into ch-3 space, ch 3 (first dc), (2 dc, ch 3, 3 dc) into same ch-3 space, *[skip 3 sts, work 3 dc between 3rd and 4th sts] 35 times, (3 dc, ch 3, 3 dc) into ch-3 space, [skip 3 sts, work 3 dc between 3rd and 4th sts] 6 times*, (3 dc, ch 3, 3 dc) into ch-3 space, repeat from * to * one time, Sl st into top of first dc to join—282 sts; 270 dc + 4 ch-3 spaces.

Round 9: Sl st into each of next 2 dc, Sl st into ch-3 space, ch 3 (first dc), (2 dc, ch 3, 3 dc) into same ch-3 space, *[skip 3 sts, work 3 dc between 3rd and 4th sts] 36 times, (3 dc, ch 3, 3 dc) into ch-3 space, [skip 3 sts, work 3 dc between 3rd and 4th sts] 7 times*, (3 dc, ch 3, 3 dc) into ch-3 space, repeat from * to * one time, Sl st into top of first dc to join—294 sts; 282 dc + 4 ch-3 spaces.

Round 10: Sl st into each of next 2 dc, Sl st into ch-3 space, fasten off Color B, with Color C ch 3 (first dc), (2 dc, ch 3, 3 dc) into same ch-3 space, *[skip 3 sts, work 3 dc between 3rd and 4th sts] 37 times, (3 dc, ch 3, 3 dc) into ch-3 space, [skip 3 sts, work 3 dc between 3rd and 4th sts] 8 times*, (3 dc, ch 3, 3 dc) into ch-3 space, repeat from * to * one time, Sl st into top of first dc to join—306 sts; 294 dc + 4 ch-3 spaces.

Round 11: Sl st into each of next 2 dc, Sl st into ch-3 space, ch 3 (first dc), (2 dc, ch 3, 3 dc) into same ch-3 space, *[skip 3 sts, work 3 dc between 3rd and 4th sts] 38 times, (3 dc, ch 3, 3 dc) into ch-3 space, [skip 3 sts, work 3 dc between 3rd and 4th sts] 9 times*, (3 dc, ch 3, 3 dc) into ch-3 space, repeat from * to * one time, Sl st into top of first dc to join—318 sts; 306 dc + 4 ch-3 spaces.

Round 12 (Rectangles 1 and 2): Sl st into each of next 2 dc, Sl st into ch-3 space, ch 3 (first dc), (2 dc, ch 3, 3 dc) into same ch-3 space, *[skip 3 sts, work 3 dc between 3rd and 4th sts] 39 times, (3 dc, ch 3, 3 dc) into ch-3 space, [skip 3 sts, work 3 dc between 3rd and 4th sts] 10 times*, (3 dc, ch 3, 3 dc) into ch-3 space, repeat from * to * one time, Sl st into top of first dc to join, fasten off—330 sts; 318 dc + 4 ch-3 spaces.

Work Rectangle Foundation and Rectangle instructions 3 times, completing 2 Rectangles through Round 12 (above) and stopping at Round 11 for the third

Rectangle (which will be joined to the first and second Rectangles in the following round). Ensure all Rectangles are joined with the right sides facing the same direction.

Round 12 (Rectangle 3 only): Sl st into each of next 2 dc, Sl st into ch-3 space, ch 3 (first dc), (2 dc, ch 1, Sl st into ch-3 space of Rectangle 1, ch 1, 3 dc) into same ch-3 space, [skip 3 sts in Rectangle 1, Sl st between 3rd and 4th sts, skip 3 sts in Rectangle 3, work 3 dc between 3rd and 4th sts] 39 times, skip 3 sts in Rectangle 1, Sl st between 3rd and 4th sts, (3 dc, ch 1, Sl st into ch-3 space of Rectangle 1, ch 1, 3 dc) into ch-3 space, [skip 3 sts, work 3 dc between 3rd and 4th sts] 10 times, (3 dc, ch 1, Sl st into ch-3 space of Rectangle 2, ch 1, 3 dc) into same ch-3 space, [skip 3 sts in Rectangle 2, Sl st between 3rd and 4th sts, skip 3 sts in Rectangle 3, work 3 dc between 3rd and 4th sts] 39 times, skip 3 sts in Rectangle 2, Sl st between 3rd and 4th sts, (3 dc, ch 1, Sl st into ch-3 space of Rectangle 2, ch 1, 3 dc) into ch-3 space, [skip 3 sts, work 3 dc between 3rd and 4th sts] 10 times, Sl st into top of first dc to join, fasten off—406 sts; 318 dc + 80 Sl sts + 8 ch.

Double-Knot Fringe

1. Cut 8 strands of yarn measuring 20 in./50.75 cm each (1 bundle). Make 40 bundles to distribute across the 2 joined ends of Throw (20 bundles per side). Repeat for each side:
2. Evenly knot 1 bundle into upper left ch-3 space of Rectangle 1, [skip 6 sts, knot 1 bundle] 6 times.
3. Evenly knot 1 bundle into upper right ch-3 space of Rectangle 2, [skip 6 sts, knot 1 bundle] 6 times.
4. Working across Rectangle 3, evenly knot 1 bundle after first 3 dc in upper right corner, [skip 6 sts, knot 1 bundle] 5 times.
5. Double Knot:
   - Knot whole bundle on far right with half bundle on immediate left (1 in./2.5 cm from first knot).
   - Knot whole bundle on far left with half bundle on immediate right (1 in./2.5 cm from first knot).
   - Separate half of all remaining bundles, knot adjacent bundles together (1 in./2.5 cm from first attachment knot)

Finishing
Sew in all ends, trim excess.

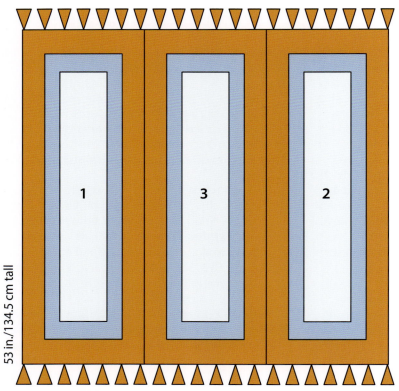
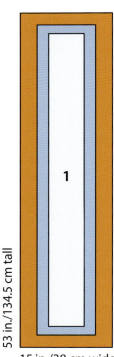

45 in./114.25 cm wide

15 in./38 cm wide

Granny Scrap Throw

Because granny squares are typically made with scrap yarn, this is the perfect scrappy throw blanket! The design starts with traditional granny square motifs to form the blanket's length (shown in Pale Grey/Bluestone). Next, width is asymmetrically added to both sides using a granny stitch (shown in Rose/Dusty Rose), and it's all finished off with a granny stitch border around the edge (shown in Cream/Mustard).

YARN
Lion Brand Pound of Love, medium #4 (80% premium acrylic; 1,020 yds./932 m per 16 oz./454 g skein)
Color A: Sugar Cookie, 2 skeins

Lion Brand Scarfie, bulky #5 (78% acrylic, 22% wool; 312 yds./285 m per 5.3 oz./150 g skein)
Color B: Pale Grey/Bluestone, 2 skeins
Color C: Rose/Dusty Rose, 3 skeins
Color D: Cream/Mustard, 1 skein

TOOLS
US size K/10.5 (6.5 mm) crochet hook
Yarn needle

GAUGE
1 Granny Square = 13 in./33 cm square
10 pattern rows = 7.25 in./18.5 cm
11 pattern sts = 4 in./10.25 cm

FINISHED SIZE
52 in./132 cm across x 56 in./142 cm tall (with border)

SPECIALTY STITCH
JAYGO (join as you go): Replace 1 chain stitch with 1 slip stitch into the joining motif.

PATTERN NOTES
- Pattern is worked with two strands of yarn (Pound of Love, Scarfie) held together for all sections.
- Pattern is worked in sections: Granny Squares (rounds), Blanket (Parts 1 and 2; rows), Border (rounds).

INSTRUCTIONS

Granny Square 1

Round 1 (right side): With Colors A and B held together ch 4 (first dc and base ch), 2 dc, [ch 3, 3 dc] 3 times into 4th ch from hook, ch 3, Sl st into top of beginning ch-3 to join—24 sts; 12 dc + 4 ch-3 spaces.

Round 2: Sl st into each of next 2 dc, Sl st into ch-3 space, ch 3 (first dc, here and throughout), (2 dc, ch 3, 3 dc) into same ch-3 space, ch 1, [(3 dc, ch 3, 3 dc) into next ch-3 space, ch 1] 3 times, Sl st into top of beginning ch-3 to join—40 sts; 24 dc + 4 ch-3 spaces + 4 ch-1 spaces.

Round 3: Sl st into each of next 2 dc, Sl st into ch-3 space, (ch 3, 2 dc, ch 3, 3 dc) into same ch-3 space, ch 1, (3 dc, ch 1) into ch-1 space, [(3 dc, ch 3, 3 dc) into next ch-3 space, ch 1, (3 dc, ch 1) into ch-1 space] 3 times, Sl st into top of beginning ch-3 to join—56 sts; 36 dc + 4 ch-3 spaces + 8 ch-1 spaces.

Round 4: Sl st into each of next 2 dc, Sl st into ch-3 space, (ch 3, 2 dc, ch 3, 3 dc) into same ch-3 space, ch 1, (3 dc, ch 1) into each ch-1 space, [(3 dc, ch 3, 3 dc) into next ch-3 space, ch 1, (3 dc, ch 1) into each ch-1 space] 3 times, Sl st into top of beginning ch-3 to join—72 sts; 48 dc + 4 ch-3 spaces + 12 ch-1 spaces.

Repeat Round 4 until 8 rounds are complete, adding 16 sts to each new round of work, ending with 136 sts; 96 dc + 4 ch-3 spaces + 28 ch. Fasten off.

Granny Squares 2–4

Follow instructions for Granny Square 1 through Round 7, then continue to Round 8 below to join the first side of the current Granny Square to the third side of the previous Granny Square (joining all squares into a straight line). Ensure all squares are joined with the right side facing the same direction.

Round 8: Follow instructions for Round 4, except replace 2nd ch along 2 consecutive ch-3 spaces, and each ch-1 space between those spaces, with JAYGO, fasten off—136 sts; 96 dc + 9 Sl sts + 2 ch-3 spaces + 2 ch-2 corners with Sl st + 21 ch-1 spaces.

Blanket

Part 1

With the right side of Granny Squares 1–4 facing, turn to work into sides of squares beginning with the far right ch-3 space.

Row 1 (right side): With Colors A and C ch 3 (first dc here and throughout), work 2 dc into same ch-3 space, (ch 1, 3 dc) into each ch-1 space and ch-3 joined space across all 4 Granny Squares—143 sts; 108 dc + 35 ch.

Row 2: Ch 3, turn, (ch 1, 3 dc) into each ch-1 space across row, (ch 1, dc) into top of last st—143 sts; 107 dc + 36 ch.

Row 3: Ch 3, turn, work 2 dc into same ch-1 space, (ch 1, 3 dc) into each ch-1 space across row—143 sts; 108 dc + 35 ch.

Repeat Rows 2 and 3 until 40 rows are complete. Fasten off.

Part 2
With the right side of Granny Squares 1–4 facing, turn to work into sides of squares (opposite Part 1), beginning with the far right ch-3 space.

Row 1 (right side): With Colors A and C ch 3 (first dc here and throughout), work 2 dc into same ch-3 space, (ch 1, 3 dc) into each ch-1 space and ch-3 joined space across all 4 Granny Squares—143 sts; 108 dc + 35 ch.

Row 2: Ch 3, turn, (ch 1, 3 dc) into each ch-1 space across row, (ch 1, dc) into top of last st—143 sts; 107 dc + 36 ch.

Row 3: Ch 3, turn, work 2 dc into same ch-1 space, (ch 1, 3 dc) into each ch-1 space across row—143 sts; 108 dc + 35 ch.

Repeat Rows 2 and 3 until 8 rows are complete. Fasten off.

Border
With the right side of Granny Squares 1–4 facing, join yarn into far right ch-1 space in last row of Part 2.

Round 1 (right side): With Colors A and D ch 3 (first dc, here and throughout), (2 dc, ch 3, 3 dc) into same space, (ch 1, 3 dc) into each ch-1 space across last row of Part 2, ch 3 at row end, turn to work into sides of Part 2/Granny Square/Part 1. *(3 dc, ch 1) into: side of each odd row of Part 2 and Part 1, ch-3 corner and ch-1 space across Granny Square*. Ch 3 at side end, turn to work into last row of Part 1. (3 dc, ch 1) into each ch-1 space across last row of Part 1. Ch 3 at row end, turn to work into sides of Part 1/Granny Square/Part 2. Repeat from * to * once more, Sl st into top of first dc to join—560 sts; 414 dc + 134 ch + 4 ch-3 spaces.

Round 2: Sl st into each of next 2 dc, sl st into ch-3 space, (ch 3, 2 dc, ch 3, 3 dc) into same ch-3 space, (ch 1, 3 dc) into each ch-1 space in round, (ch 1, 3 dc, ch 3, 3 dc) into each ch-3 space, Sl st into top of first dc to join—576 sts; 426 dc + 138 ch + 4 ch-3 spaces.

Repeat Round 2 one more time; 3 complete rounds. Fasten off. 592 sts; 438 dc + 142 ch + 4 ch-3 spaces.

Finishing
Sew in all ends, trim excess.

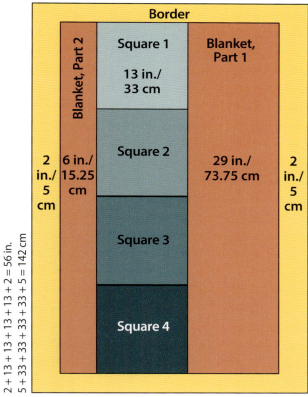

2 + 6 + 13 + 29 + 2 = 52 in.
5 + 15.25 + 33 + 73.75 + 5 = 132 cm

Granny Square Reflections Throw

This throw might look like a typical granny square at first glance, but it's actually two rectangular motifs that are seamed together! To make the design really stand out, each rectangle is worked in contrasting colors, giving it a fresh and eye-catching twist.

YARN
Lion Brand Re-Spun Thick & Quick, super bulky #6 (100% recycled polyester; 223 yds./204 m per 12 oz./340 g skein)
Color A: Pumice Stone, 2 skeins
Color B: Squash, 1 skein
Color C: Wisteria, 2 skeins
Color D: Dark Cherry, 1 skein

TOOLS
US size N/15 (10 mm) crochet hook
Stitch markers (to mark stitches, as desired)
Yarn needle

GAUGE
4 pattern rows = 4 in./10.25 cm
1 Rectangle = 52 in./132 cm across (sts) x 26 in./66 cm tall (rows)

FINISHED SIZE
52 in./132 cm x 52 in./132 cm (without fringe)

SPECIALTY TECHNIQUE
Sew (whipstitch): With yarn needle, evenly join (sew) fabric together.

PATTERN NOTES
- Throw is worked by creating two Rectangles (rows) that are joined together with Seams (rows/sewing) once complete.
- The contrasting colors help to feature the construction of the individual pieces.

24

INSTRUCTIONS

Rectangles (Make 2)
Rectangle 1: Rows 1–16 = Color A, Rows 17–23 = Color B, Rows 24–26 = Color C, Seam = Color C, Fringe = Color A

Rectangle 2: Rows 1–16 = Color C, Rows 17–23 = Color D, Rows 24–26 = Color A, Seam = Color A, Fringe = Color C

Row 1: Ch 4 (first dc, base ch), (2 dc, ch 3, 3 dc, ch 3, 3 dc) into 4th ch from hook—15 sts; 9 dc + 6 ch.

Row 2: Ch 4 (first dc + ch-1 here and throughout), turn, (3 dc, ch 3, 3 dc, ch 1) into each of next 2 ch-3 spaces, dc into top of last st—23 sts; 14 dc + 9 ch.

Row 3: Ch 3, turn, (2 dc, ch 1) into ch-1 space, (3 dc, ch 3, 3 dc, ch 1) into ch-3 space, (3 dc, ch 1) into ch-1 space, (3 dc, ch 3, 3 dc, ch 1) into ch-3 space, 3 dc into ch-1 space—31 sts; 21 dc + 10 ch.

Row 4: Ch 4, turn, (3 dc, ch 1) into each ch-1 space across first side, (3 dc, ch 3, 3 dc, ch 1) into ch-3 space, (3 dc, ch 1) into each ch-1 space across second side, (3 dc, ch 3, 3 dc, ch 1) into ch-3 space, (3 dc, ch 1) into each ch-1 space across third side, dc into top of last st—39 sts; 26 dc + 13 ch.

Row 5: Ch 3, turn, (2 dc, ch 1) into ch-1 space, (3 dc, ch 1) into each ch-1 space across first side, (3 dc, ch 3, 3 dc, ch 1) into ch-3 space, (3 dc, ch 1) into each ch-1 space across second side, (3 dc, ch 3, 3 dc, ch 1) into ch-3 space, (3 dc, ch 1) into each ch-1 space across third side, except work 3 dc into last ch-1 space—47 sts; 33 dc + 14 ch.

Repeat Rows 4 and 5 until 26 rows are complete (ending on a Row 4 repeat). Do not fasten off, continue to Seams.

Seams
Rotate to work into sides of rows from Rectangle.

Row 1 (right side): Ch 1 (not a st), work 2 sc around each row end from Rectangle—104 sc.

Fasten off 60 in./152.5 cm yarn tail for Rectangle 1 only. When both Rectangles are complete, hold Seams together with right sides facing the same direction. Thread 60 in./152.5 cm yarn tail into yarn needle, evenly sew Seams together, fasten off.

Double-Knot Fringe
1. Cut 4 strands of yarn measuring 20 in./50.75 cm each (1 bundle). Make 27 bundles for each Rectangle.
2. Evenly knot 1 bundle into both ch-3 spaces in Row 26, then knot remaining bundles between them (along 2nd side of Rectangle).
3. Double knot:
   a. Knot whole bundle on far right with half bundle on the immediate left, about 1 in./2.5 cm from the first knot.
   b. Knot whole bundle on far left with half bundle on the immediate right, about 1 in./2.5 cm from the first knot.
   c. Separate half of all remaining bundles and knot adjacent bundles together about 1 in./2.5 cm from first attachment knot.

Finishing
Sew in all ends, trim excess.

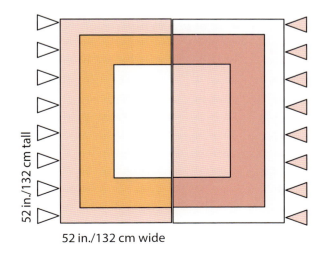

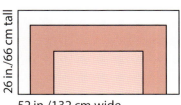

GRANNY SQUARE REFLECTIONS THROW

Granny Triangles Throw

This circular throw is crafted by joining six separate triangle motifs, each worked using the classic granny stitch. By switching yarn colors for the final round of each motif and the outer edge of the throw, you can highlight the distinctly different construction.

YARN
Lion Brand Wool Ease Thick & Quick, super bulky #6 (80% acrylic, 20% wool
Color A: Fisherman, 6 skeins (106 yds./97 m per 6 oz./170 g skein)
Color B: Driftwood, 6 skeins (87 yds./80 m per 5 oz./140 g skein)

TOOLS
US size N/15 (10 mm) crochet hook
Stitch markers (to mark stitches, as desired)
Yarn needle

GAUGE
1 Triangle = 27 in./68.5 cm tall x 27 in./68.5 cm wide

FINISHED SIZE
Without Border: 54 in./137.25 cm across
Border adds 3 in./7.5 cm to total measurements

SPECIALTY STITCH
BLO: Work into the back loop only of a stitch.

PATTERN NOTES
- Throw is worked by creating 6 individual Triangles (rounds) that are crocheted together with Seams (rows) once complete. A border (rounds) is added last.
- The contrasting colors help to feature the construction of the individual triangles.

INSTRUCTIONS

Triangle (make 6)

Round 1 (right side): With Color A ch 4 (first dc, base ch), (3 dc, ch 3, 4 dc, ch 3, 4 dc, ch 3) into 4th ch from hook, Sl st into top of first dc to join—21 sts; 12 dc + 3 ch-3 spaces.

Round 2: Sl st into each of next 4 sts, ch 3 (first dc, here and throughout), (3 dc, ch 3, 4 dc, ch 1) into ch-3 space, (4 dc, ch 3, 4 dc, ch 1) into each of next 2 ch-3 spaces, Sl st into top of first dc to join—36 sts; 24 dc + 3 ch-3 spaces + 3 ch-1 spaces.

Round 3: Sl st into each of next 4 sts, (ch 3, 3 dc, ch 3, 4 dc, ch 1) into ch-3 space, (4 dc, ch 1) into ch-1 space, [(4 dc, ch 3, 4 dc, ch 1) into ch-3 space, (4 dc, ch 1) into ch-1 space] 2 times, Sl st into top of first dc to join—51 sts; 36 dc + 3 ch-3 spaces + 6 ch-1 spaces.

Round 4: Sl st into each of next 4 sts, (ch 3, 3 dc, ch 3, 4 dc, ch 1) into ch-3 space, (4 dc, ch 1) into next 2 ch-1 spaces, [(4 dc, ch 3, 4 dc, ch 1) into ch-3 space, (4 dc, ch 1) into next 2 ch-1 spaces] 2 times, Sl st into top of first dc to join—66 sts; 48 dc + 3 ch-3 spaces + 9 ch-1 spaces.

Round 5: Sl st into each of next 4 sts, (ch 3, 3 dc, ch 3, 4 dc, ch 1) into ch-3 space, (4 dc, ch 1) into next 3 ch-1 spaces, [(4 dc, ch 3, 4 dc, ch 1) into ch-3 space, (4 dc, ch 1) into next 3 ch-1 spaces] 2 times, Sl st into top of first dc to join—81 sts; 60 dc + 3 ch-3 spaces + 12 ch-1 spaces.

Round 6: Sl st into each of next 4 sts, (ch 3, 3 dc, ch 3, 4 dc, ch 1) into ch-3 space, (4 dc, ch 1) into next 4 ch-1 spaces, [(4 dc, ch 3, 4 dc, ch 1) into ch-3 space, (4 dc, ch 1) into next 4 ch-1 spaces] 2 times, Sl st into top of first dc to join—96 sts; 72 dc + 3 ch-3 spaces + 15 ch-1 spaces.

Round 7: Sl st into each of next 4 sts, (ch 3, 3 dc, ch 3, 4 dc, ch 1) into ch-3 space, (4 dc, ch 1) into next 5 ch-1 spaces, [(4 dc, ch 3, 4 dc, ch 1) into ch-3 space, (4 dc, ch 1) into next 5 ch-1 spaces] 2 times, Sl st into top of first dc to join—111 sts; 84 dc + 3 ch-3 spaces + 18 ch-1 spaces.

Round 8: Sl st into each of next 4 sts, fasten off Color A, with Color B (ch 3, 3 dc, ch 3, 4 dc, ch 1) into ch-3 space, (4 dc, ch 1) into next 6 ch-1 spaces, [(4 dc, ch 3, 4 dc, ch 1) into ch-3 space, (4 dc, ch 1) into next 6 ch-1 spaces] 2 times, Sl st into top of first dc to join—126 sts; 96 dc + 3 ch-3 spaces + 21 ch-1 spaces.

Round 9: Sl st into each of next 4 sts, (ch 3, 3 dc, ch 3, 4 dc, ch 1) into ch-3 space, (4 dc, ch 1) into next 7 ch-1 spaces, [(4 dc, ch 3, 4 dc, ch 1) into ch-3 space, (4 dc, ch 1) into next 7 ch-1 spaces] 2 times, Sl st into top of first dc to join, fasten off—141 sts; 108 dc + 3 ch-3 spaces + 24 ch-1 spaces.

Seams

With right sides of all Triangles facing the same direction, arrange together to form a hexagon/circle.

Seam 1

Attach Color B into BLO of second chs in outermost (not in center of circle) ch-3 corners for Triangles 1 and 2.

Row 1 (right side): Sl st into BLO of both thicknesses until second ch of next ch-3 is reached (48 Sl st), ch 1, Sl st into BLO of both thicknesses of second chs in ch-3 corners for Triangles 4 and 5, Sl st into BLO of both thicknesses until second ch of next ch-3 is reached (48 Sl sts), fasten off—97 sts; 96 Sl st + 1 ch.

Seam 2

Attach Color B into BLO of second chs in outermost (not in center of circle) ch-3 corners for Triangles 2 and 3.

Row 1 (right side): Sl st into BLO of both thicknesses until second ch of next ch-3 is reached (48 Sl st), ch 1, Sl st into BLO of both thicknesses of second chs in ch-3 corners for Triangles 5 and 6, Sl st into BLO of both thicknesses until second ch of next ch-3 is reached (48 Sl sts), fasten off—97 sts; 96 Sl st + 1 ch.

Seam 3
Attach Color B into BLO of second chs in outermost (not in center of circle) ch-3 corners for Triangles 3 and 4.

Row 1 (right side): Sl st into BLO of both thicknesses until second ch of next ch-3 is reached (48 Sl st), ch 1, Sl st into BLO of both thicknesses of second chs in ch-3 corners for Triangles 1 and 6, Sl st into BLO of both thicknesses until second ch of next ch-3 is reached (48 Sl sts), fasten off—97 sts; 96 Sl st + 1 ch.

Border
With right sides of Seams facing, attach Color B into last Sl st of any Seam.

Round 1 (right side): Ch 3 (first dc), (dc, ch 3, 2 dc) into same st, [skip 1 dc, sc into next 2 sts, skip 1 dc, *[(2 dc, ch 3, 2 dc) into next ch-1 space] 8 times, skip 1 dc, sc into next 2 sts, skip 1 dc (2 dc, ch 3, 2 dc) into last Sl st of next Seam*, repeat from * to * 5 times, [skip 1 dc, sc into next 2 sts, skip 1 dc (2 dc, ch 3, 2 dc)] 8 times, Sl st into top of first st to join, fasten off—486 sts; 216 dc + 54 ch-3 spaces + 108 sc.

Finishing
Sew in all ends, trim excess.

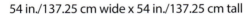

54 in./137.25 cm wide x 54 in./137.25 cm tall

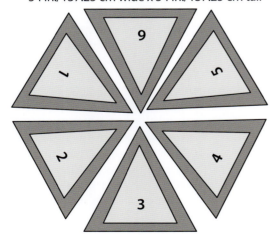

27 in./68.5 cm tall

27 in./68.5 cm wide

Lazy Days Throw

If you're into granny squares, this design will be your new favorite. It looks a lot like the classic, but here's the twist: you'll crochet four triangles (yes, triangles!) and join them together to form a square. But remember, those contrasting colors help to show the unique construction—not at all like your grandma's granny square!

YARN
Lion Brand Cover Story Lazy Days Thick & Quick, super bulky #6 (100% polyester; 125 yds./114 m per 8.8 oz./250 g skein)
Color A: Amber, 4 skeins
Color B: Cream, 5 skeins

TOOLS
US size M/13 (9 mm) crochet hook
Stitch markers (to mark stitches, as desired)
Yarn needle

GAUGE
1 Triangle = 45 in./114.25 cm wide x 22.5 in./57.25 cm tall

FINISHED SIZE
Without Border: 45 in./114.3 cm across square, or 64 in./162.5 cm diagonally, corner to corner
Border adds 3 in./7.5 cm to total measurements

SPECIALTY STITCH
BLO: Work into the back loop only of a stitch.

PATTERN NOTES
- Throw is worked by creating 4 individual Triangles (rows) that are crocheted together with Seams (rows) once complete. A border (rounds) is added last.
- The contrasting colors help to feature the construction, which is distinctly different from a classic granny square.

INSTRUCTIONS

Triangle (make 4)

Row 1: With Color A ch 5 (first dc, ch-1 space, base ch), (3 dc, ch 2, 3 dc, ch 1, dc) into fifth ch from hook—12 sts; 8 dc + 4 ch.

Row 2: Ch 4 (first dc and ch-1 space), turn, (3 dc, ch 1) into ch-1 space, (3 dc, ch 2, 3 dc) into ch-2 space, (ch 1, 3 dc) into ch-1 space, (ch 1, dc) into top of last st in row—20 sts; 14 dc + 6 ch.

Row 3: Ch 4, turn, (3 dc, ch 1) into next 2 ch-1 spaces, (3 dc, ch 2, 3 dc) into ch-2 space, (ch 1, 3 dc) into next 2 ch-1 spaces, (ch 1, dc) into top of last st in row—28 sts; 20 dc + 8 ch.

Row 4: Ch 4, turn, (3 dc, ch 1) into next 3 ch-1 spaces, (3 dc, ch 2, 3 dc) into ch-2 space, (ch 1, 3 dc) into next 3 ch-1 spaces, (ch 1, dc) into top of last st in row—36 sts; 26 dc + 10 ch.

Row 5: Ch 4, turn, (3 dc, ch 1) into next 4 ch-1 spaces, (3 dc, ch 2, 3 dc) into ch-2 space, (ch 1, 3 dc) into next 4 ch-1 spaces, (ch 1, dc) into top of last st in row—44 sts; 32 dc + 12 ch.

Row 6: Ch 4, turn, (3 dc, ch 1) into next 5 ch-1 spaces, (3 dc, ch 2, 3 dc) into ch-2 space, (ch 1, 3 dc) into next 5 ch-1 spaces, (ch 1, dc) into top of last st in row—52 sts; 38 dc + 14 ch.

Row 7: Ch 4, turn, (3 dc, ch 1) into next 6 ch-1 spaces, (3 dc, ch 2, 3 dc) into ch-2 space, (ch 1, 3 dc) into next 6 ch-1 spaces, (ch 1, dc) into top of last st in row—60 sts; 44 dc + 16 ch.

Row 8: Ch 4, turn, (3 dc, ch 1) into next 7 ch-1 spaces, (3 dc, ch 2, 3 dc) into ch-2 space, (ch 1, 3 dc) into next 7 ch-1 spaces, (ch 1, dc) into top of last st in row—68 sts; 50 dc + 18 ch.

Row 9: Ch 4, turn, (3 dc, ch 1) into next 8 ch-1 spaces, (3 dc, ch 2, 3 dc) into ch-2 space, (ch 1, 3 dc) into next 8 ch-1 spaces, (ch 1, dc) into top of last st in row—76 sts; 56 dc + 20 ch.

Row 10: Ch 4, turn, (3 dc, ch 1) into next 9 ch-1 spaces, (3 dc, ch 2, 3 dc) into ch-2 space, (ch 1, 3 dc) into next 9 ch-1 spaces, (ch 1, dc) into top of last st in row—84 sts; 62 dc + 22 ch.

Row 11: Ch 4, turn, (3 dc, ch 1) into next 10 ch-1 spaces, (3 dc, ch 2, 3 dc) into ch-2 space, (ch 1, 3 dc) into next 10 ch-1 spaces, (ch 1, dc) into top of last st in row—92 sts; 68 dc + 24 ch.

Row 12: Ch 4, turn, (3 dc, ch 1) into next 11 ch-1 spaces, (3 dc, ch 2, 3 dc) into ch-2 space, (ch 1, 3 dc) into next 11 ch-1 spaces, (ch 1, dc) into top of last st in row, fasten off Color A—100 sts; 74 dc + 26 ch.

Row 13: With Color B ch 4, turn, (3 dc, ch 1) into next 12 ch-1 spaces, (3 dc, ch 2, 3 dc) into ch-2 space, (ch 1, 3 dc) into next 12 ch-1 spaces, (ch 1, dc) into top of last st in row—108 sts; 80 dc + 28 ch.

Row 14: Ch 4, turn, (3 dc, ch 1) into next 13 ch-1 spaces, (3 dc, ch 2, 3 dc) into ch-2 space, (ch 1, 3 dc) into next 13 ch-1 spaces, (ch 1, dc) into top of last st in row—116 sts; 86 dc + 30 ch.

Row 15: Ch 4, turn, (3 dc, ch 1) into next 14 ch-1 spaces, (3 dc, ch 2, 3 dc) into ch-2 space, (ch 1, 3 dc) into next 14 ch-1 spaces, (ch 1, dc) into top of last st in row—124 sts; 92 dc + 32 ch.

Row 16: Ch 4, turn, (3 dc, ch 1) into next 15 ch-1 spaces, (3 dc, ch 2, 3 dc) into ch-2 space, (ch 1, 3 dc) into next 15 ch-1 spaces, (ch 1, dc) into top of last st in row—132 sts; 98 dc + 34 ch.

Row 17 (right side): Ch 4, turn, (3 dc, ch 1) into next 16 ch-1 spaces, (3 dc, ch 2, 3 dc) into ch-2 space, (ch 1, 3 dc) into next 16 ch-1 spaces, (ch 1, dc) into top of last st in row, fasten off—140 sts; 104 dc + 36 ch.

Seams

Seam 1

With right sides of all Triangles facing the same direction, align last rows together to form a square. Attach Color B into BLO of first st for one Triangle and BLO of last st for adjacent Triangle.

Row 1 (right side): Sl st into BLO of both thicknesses for first two triangles until first ch of ch-2 space is reached (70 Sl st). Starting with second ch of ch-2

spaces, Sl st into BLO of both thicknesses for next two triangles until first st for one Triangle and last st for adjacent Triangle are reached (70 Sl st), fasten off—140 Sl st.

Seam 2
With right sides of all Triangles and Seam facing the same direction, rotate to work across unjoined Triangles. Join Color B into BLO of first st for one Triangle and BLO of last st for adjacent Triangle.
Row 1 (right side): Sl st into BLO of both thicknesses for first two triangles until first ch of ch-2 space is reached (70 Sl st), ch 1. Starting with second ch of ch-2 spaces, Sl st into BLO of both thicknesses for next two triangles until first st for one Triangle and last st for adjacent Triangle are reached (70 Sl st), fasten off—141 sts; 140 Sl st + 1 ch.

Border
With right sides of Seams facing, attach Color B into side of any row end from a Triangle.
Round 1 (right side): Ch 1 (not a st, here and throughout), work 3 sc into side of each row end for each Triangle, Sl st into top of first st to join—408 sc.
Round 2: Ch 1, [sc, ch 2, skip 2 sts] around, Sl st into top of first st to join—408 sts; 136 sc + 272 ch.
Round 3: Ch 1, [sc on top of sc, (ch 1, dc, ch 1) into ch-2 space] around, Sl st into top of first st to join, fasten off—544 sts; 136 sc + 136 dc + 272 ch.

Finishing
Sew in all ends, trim excess.

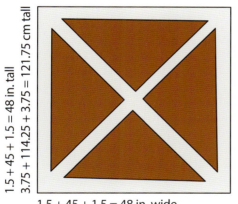

1.5 + 45 + 1.5 = 48 in. wide
3.75 + 114.25 + 3.75 = 121.75 cm wide

45 in./114.25 cm wide

LAZY DAYS THROW

Mile-a-Minute Granny Throw

Using two strands of yarn held together and a super simple granny stitch chevron repeat, each motif in this blanket feels like it works up a mile a minute! Each of the five chevron strips are worked separately, then a contrasting color is used to add a border and to join the strips.

YARN
Lion Brand Bundle of Love, medium #4 (100% acrylic; 688 yds./629 m per 11 oz./312 g skein)
Color A: Potpourri, 2 skeins
Lion Brand Jiffy, bulky #5 (100% acrylic; 681 yds./623 m per 14.5 oz./410 g skein)
Color B: Aero, 2 skeins
Color C: Cream, 1 skein

TOOLS
US size K/10.5 (6.5 mm) crochet hook
Stitch markers (to mark stitches, as desired)
Yarn needle

GAUGE
1 Granny Chevron = 9 in./23 cm wide x 53 in./134.5 cm long (without border)

FINISHED SIZE
55 in./139.75 cm wide x 55 in./139.75 cm long (with border)

PATTERN NOTES
- Throw is worked by creating 5 Granny Chevrons (rows), with a border added around each (round) once the length is complete. Finally, the motifs are crocheted together with Seams (rows) and fringe is added last.
- Granny Chevrons are worked with two strands of yarn held together. Border is worked with a single strand and determines the right side of fabric.
- The contrasting colors help to feature the construction, which is interestingly different from a solid granny chevron throw.

INSTRUCTIONS

Granny Chevron (make 5)
Row 1: With Colors A and B held together ch 28, skip 3 ch (first dc), work 1 dc into each of next 12 sts, ch 2, work 1 dc into each of last 13 sts—28 sts; 26 dc + 2 ch.
Row 2: Ch 3 (first dc), turn, *[skip 3 sts, work 3 dc between 3rd and 4th sts] 3 times*, (3 dc, ch 2, 3 dc) into ch-2 space, repeat from * to * one time, work 1 dc into top of last st—28 sts; 26 dc + 2 ch.
Repeat Row 2 until 45 rows are complete. Fasten off Colors A and B, join Color C. Continue on to Border.

Border
When working Round 1 of the Border, place 1 st marker into each ch-1 space (4 total) to help mark joins for Seams.
Round 1 (right side): Ch 3 (first dc), turn, work 2 dc into same st, *[skip 3 sts, work 3 dc between 3rd and 4th sts] 3 times*, (3 dc, ch 2, 3 dc) into ch-2 space, repeat from * to * one time, work 3 dc into top of last st. **Rotate to work into sides of Granny Chevron rows. Ch 1, work 3 dc into side of each Granny Chevron row (45 total rows). Rotate to work into Row 1. Ch 1**, skip 1 st, work 3 dc between 2nd and 3rd sts, [skip 3 sts, work 3 dc between 3rd and 4th sts] 3 times, skip 3 sts, work 1 dc between 3rd and 4th sts, repeat from * to * one time, skip 3 sts, work 3 dc between 3rd and 4th sts. Repeat from ** to ** one time, Sl st into top of first st to join, fasten off—331 sts; 325 dc + 6 ch.

Seam
Align all Granny Chevrons so that their sides are touching, with first rows pointing on one side and last rows pointing on the other. Assure right sides are all facing the same direction.
Follow Row 1 of Seam instructions to join Granny Chevron 1 to 2, 3 to 2, 4 to 3, and 5 to 4.
Working through both pieces of fabric, join Color C into ch-1 spaces nearest the last row of Granny Chevron.
Row 1 (right side): Ch 1 (not a st), sc into ch-1 space, [ch 2, skip 3 sts, sc between sts] 44 times, (ch 2, sc) into ch-1 space, fasten off—136 sts; 46 sc + 45 ch-2 spaces.

Fringe
For every ch-2 space (5 total), ch-1 space (2 total), and 2 adjacent ch-1 spaces (4 total) around Granny Chevron Border (see diagram):
1. Cut 20 pieces of yarn, each measuring 14 in./35.5 cm.
2. Fold in half, evenly feed and knot into ch space indicated.
3. Trim ends to make even.

Finishing
Sew in all ends, trim excess.

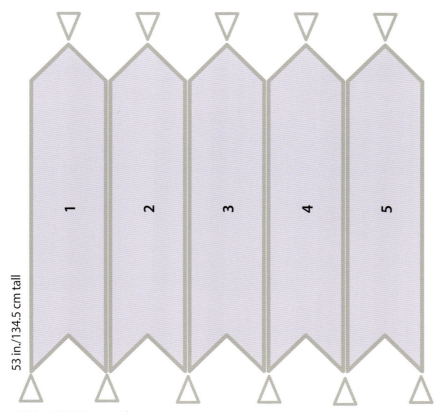

55 in./139.75 cm wide
53 in./134.5 cm tall

9 in./22.75 cm wide
53 in./134.5 cm tall

Resources

YarnSub.com—A free site where yarn substitution is made easy!

YouTube.com/AmericanCrochetAssociation—A free library of video tutorials for crochet stitches and other basics like holding your yarn and hook, the slip knot, the slip stitch, color changes, weaving and sewing in ends, and much more!

Ravelry.com/designers/salena-baca—Got a question about one of these designs, or just want to see how others have worked them up? You can find this book, and all the designs, neatly listed on Ravelry with direct access to Salena Baca!

Get started on your next crochet project with one of these great titles, also from Salena Baca:

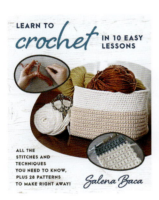 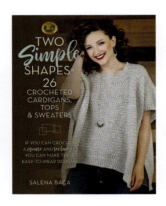 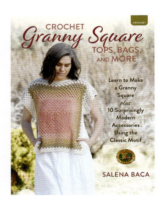 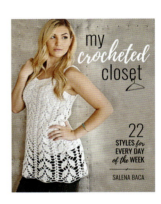

 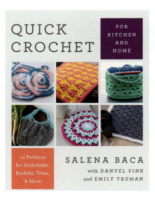